JUNIOR
BIOGRAPHIES

ED
SHEERAN

SINGER-SONGWRITER

Kristen Rajczak Nelson

Enslow Publishing
101 W. 23rd Street
Suite 240
New York, NY 10011
USA
enslow.com

WORDS TO KNOW

debut To appear for the first time.

determination A quality that makes someone keep trying to do something difficult.

EP A recording that only has a few songs on it.

experience The process of doing things and having things happen to you.

gig A musician's job; a music show.

inspire To give someone an idea to create something.

label A record company.

lyrics The words in a song.

nominate To choose someone as a possible winner of an award.

reference To mention something.

stutter A speech disorder that causes someone to repeat certain sounds.

CONTENTS

Ed Sheeran

Before Ed Sheeran was one of the biggest music stars in the world, he lived with his family in the town of Framlingham in Suffolk, England. Edward Christopher Sheeran was born on February 17, 1991, to his parents John and Imogen Sheeran. He joined an older brother, Matthew.

Ed didn't have a lot of friends when he was a kid. He often felt like an outsider. He had a lot of energy, but he wasn't good at sports. Ed also had a **stutter**, which made it hard to talk to other kids. It was also difficult for him to participate in class.

Ed Says:

"Be yourself. Embrace your quirks. Being weird is a wonderful thing."

FINDING HIS PASSION

Ed's father didn't think he worked hard enough in school. So, he tried to find something for Ed to care about. From a young age, Ed played guitar and sang in the choir at school. His dad took him to see musicians like

Ed grew up in Framlingham, in Suffolk, England.

Bob Dylan and Damien Rice, hoping this would inspire him. It did! Ed wanted to make music, but he also wanted to show his father that he could work hard at something.

GETTING SERIOUS

In 2005, Ed put out his first recorded EP, *The Orange Room EP*, and his first album, *The Spinning Man*. Two years later, he put out another EP called *Want Some?* By then, he was practicing and writing songs every day. He says he never took a day off: "It comes from my dad thinking I was lazy and wanting to prove a point." When Ed was sixteen, he left high school to become a full-time musician.

To overcome his stutter, Ed rapped along with Eminem's *Marshall Mathers LP*.

CHAPTER 2
BIG CITY, BIG DREAMS

With dreams of performing his own music, Ed moved to London around 2008. He was playing music shows as much as he could. He didn't have a place of his own to live, but mostly stayed with friends or people he met at his gigs. Sometimes, he wouldn't have a place to stay and would sleep outside—including near Buckingham Palace!

During this time, Ed tried to work with other music artists, even those who didn't make the same kind of music as he did, such as those in hip hop and grime. One even featured Ed on his YouTube channel!

Ed Says:
"I was always out searching for a gig to do or a session to be in or a sofa to sleep on."

Ed plays a show at Stratford Circus in London in 2010.

A Big Break

Between 2008 and 2010, Ed put out several EPs. By now, he was well known around the London music scene. In April 2010, Ed traveled to Los Angeles, California. He tried to find any gig he could, and he was seen by actor Jamie Foxx's manager. Ed was invited on Foxx's radio show and then to stay at his house! By the end of the year, Ed had been signed by Asylum Records, a label that specializes in singer-songwriters.

Jamie Foxx (*right*) helped Ed make it big in the United States.

Ed opened for the band
Snow Patrol on their tour
in 2012.

HITTING IT BIG

In May 2011, Ed released his first major album with Asylum, called + (*Plus*). The first single, "The A Team," hit US radio in 2012. It stayed on the Billboard Top 100 for twenty-six weeks, reaching number sixteen in January 2013.

"The A Team" was nominated for Best British Single at the 2012 Brit Awards and for Song of the Year at the Grammy Awards.

CHAPTER 3
TOURING, TAYLOR, AND "THINKING OUT LOUD"

In 2013, Ed got an even bigger break—opening for 66 dates of Taylor Swift's tour for the album *Red*. It was Ed's longest tour so far and his first time playing huge, sold-out stadiums. On the tour, Ed and Taylor played the song they cowrote, "Everything Has Changed," every night. They became such close friends that Taylor once said that Ed was the "James Taylor to my Carole King," a **reference** to another pair of famous singer-songwriters.

Ed Says:

"**Write exactly what you feel. Do not tamper with the truth. Just stick it out and people will hear the emotion in a song.**"

Ed's close friendship with Taylor Swift began while the two performed together on her *Red* tour.

BEHIND THE MUSIC

Ed was only twenty-two years old while on the *Red* tour. He had many new **experiences** and even dated some of Taylor's friends. He wrote songs about what he went through—more than enough for another album. Ed is known for his ability to write an extraordinary number of songs. He says that some songs take twenty minutes

Ed gives an interview while on tour in Scotland in 2014.

to write and others take a day. Ed uses very specific references in his song **lyrics**, like the Doritos in "Don't," that he believes help him connect with his audience.

ANOTHER HIT

Ed released his next album, *x* (*Multiply*), in 2014. It **debuted** at number one on the Billboard 200 and sold 210,000 albums in its first week. In 2015, it was nominated for two Grammy Awards. "Thinking Out Loud," the

Ed has written songs for One Direction, The Weeknd, Usher, Major Lazer, and many more!

third single from the album, became his biggest hit yet. It was a number one song all over the world and won 2016 Grammy Awards for Song of the Year and Best Pop Solo Performance. By 2016, Ed was one of the biggest music acts in the world.

Ed accepts the Grammy Award for Best Pop Solo Performance for "Thinking Out Loud" in 2016.

Ed was selling out tour dates and being photographed everywhere he went. He had written one of the biggest hits of the year, "Love Yourself," performed by Justin Bieber. He decided to take time off to travel the world. He went to Japan, Iceland, and even Ghana. The long vacation gave him plenty of inspiration for future songs.

NEW HEIGHTS

Ed's third album, ÷ (*Divide*), came out on March 3, 2017, debuting at number one. The first two singles, "Shape of You" and "Castle on the Hill," were released together

In July 2015, Ed sold out three nights in a row at Wembley Stadium in London, which seats 90,000 people!

in January and immediately topped the singles charts. "Shape of You" broke the record for the most weeks spent in the top five of the Billboard Hot 100. The ÷ (*Divide*) tour began soon after the album came out and would take him all over the world through 2018.

LOOKING TO THE FUTURE

Ed already has ideas that will keep him in the spotlight for years to come. He has a plan for seven more albums and has album sales goals he wants to meet. When he was

Ed takes time for selfies and autographs with some of his fans in Sydney, Australia.

Ed supports many important charities. He has played several benefits for Teenage Cancer Trust.

named to the 2017 *Time* 100, Taylor Swift wrote about his **determination**: "He's like a fighter who pops back up on his feet before you even noticed he'd been knocked down."

Ed's unique style of music always leaves his fans wanting more.

Ed Says:

"I need something in my songs that no one has ever heard before. So, when people hear it they say, 'That's an Ed song.'"

In 2017, the Songwriters Hall of Fame honored Ed with an award especially for young songwriters making a statement in music. It's clear that in the music world, Ed's success is just beginning.

TIMELINE

1991 Ed Sheeran is born on February 17 in West Yorkshire, England.

2005 Records *The Orange Room* EP and *The Spinning Man*.

2008 Leaves school and moves to London.

2010 Travels to Los Angeles; signs a deal with Asylum Records.

2011 *+ (Plus)* is released.

2014 *x (Multiply)* is released. Ed is nominated for Best New Artist and Song of the Year at the Grammy Awards.

2015 Is nominated for Album of the Year, Best Pop Vocal Album, and Best Song Written for a Movie at the Grammy Awards.

2016 Wins Grammy Awards for Song of the Year and Best Pop Solo Performance.

2017 *÷ (Divide)* is released.

LEARN MORE

BOOKS

Gagne, Tammy. *Ed Sheeran*. Hallandale, FL: Mitchell Lane Publishers, 2017.

MacKay, Jenny. *The Art of Songwriting*. Detroit, MI: Lucent Books, 2014.

Morreale, Marie. *Ed Sheeran*. New York, NY: Scholastic, 2014.

WEBSITES

Ed Sheeran

www.edsheeran.com

Find out the latest news and tour dates for Ed Sheeran.

Ed Sheeran on SoundCloud

soundcloud.com/edsheeran

Check out many of Ed's famous tracks for free here.

INDEX

Published in 2019 by Enslow Publishing, LLC.

101 W. 23rd Street, Suite 240, New York, NY 10011
Copyright © 2019 by Enslow Publishing, LLC.

Library of Congress Cataloging-in-Publication Data

Names: Rajczak Nelson, Kristen, author.
Title: Ed Sheeran : singer-songwriter / Kristen Rajczak Nelson.
Description: New York, NY : Enslow Publishing, 2019. | Series: Junior biographies |
  Includes bibliographical references and index. | Audience: Grades 3 to 6.
Identifiers: LCCN 2017045157| ISBN 9780766097278 (library bound) | ISBN 9780766097285 (pbk.) |
  ISBN 9780766097292 (6 pack)
Subjects: LCSH: Sheeran, Ed, 1991–Juvenile literature. | Singers–England–Biography–Juvenile literature.
Classification: LCC ML3930.S484 R35 2019 | DDC 782.42164092–dc23
LC record available at https://lccn.loc.gov/2017045157

Printed in the United States of America

Photo Credits: Cover, pp. 1, JB Lacroix/WireImage/Getty Images; p. 4 Noam Galai/WireImage/Getty Images; p. 6 Great Estates/Alamy Stock Photo; p. 9 PYMCA/Universal Images Group/Getty Images; p. 10 Lester Cohen/WireImage/Getty Images; p. 13 Gareth Cattermole/TAS/Getty Images; p. 14 Tristan Fewings/Getty Images; p. 16 Alberto E. Rodriguez/WireImage/Getty Images; p. 18 Mark Metcalfe/Getty Images; p. 19 Yui Mok/PA Images/Getty Images; p. 20 Ian Gavan/Getty Images; interior page bottoms (abstract music design) Incomible/Shutterstock.com.